The Teacher Handbook

Tales of a First-Year Teacher

Supplementary Exercises

ISBN-13: 978-1-7326967-3-0

Characters and events referenced in this book are fictitious and
yield from the novel, *Tales of a First-Year Teacher*.
Any similarity to real persons, living or dead, is coincidental
and not intended by the author. Names, characters, and places are
products of the author's imagination.

This handbook is intended to be a supplement to the novel,
Tales of a First-Year Teacher.

Editing by: J.D. Parks
First Printed: October 2019

Published by: Parks Publishing & Consulting Company, LLC
P.O. Box 66
Olive Branch, MS 38654

For author booking:

contact@jdparks.com
parkspublishingcompanyllc@gmail.com

Why You Need The Teacher Handbook

Largely centered on information necessary for new and veteran teachers to navigate, the sometimes, rocky waters of day-to-day school operations and the case study novel, *Tales of a First-Year Teacher,* this in-depth workbook and journal targets four discrete areas to promote teacher reflection and assist teachers in building a positive, student-centered school environment. The four primary categories that work as the guide for this workbook are as follows:

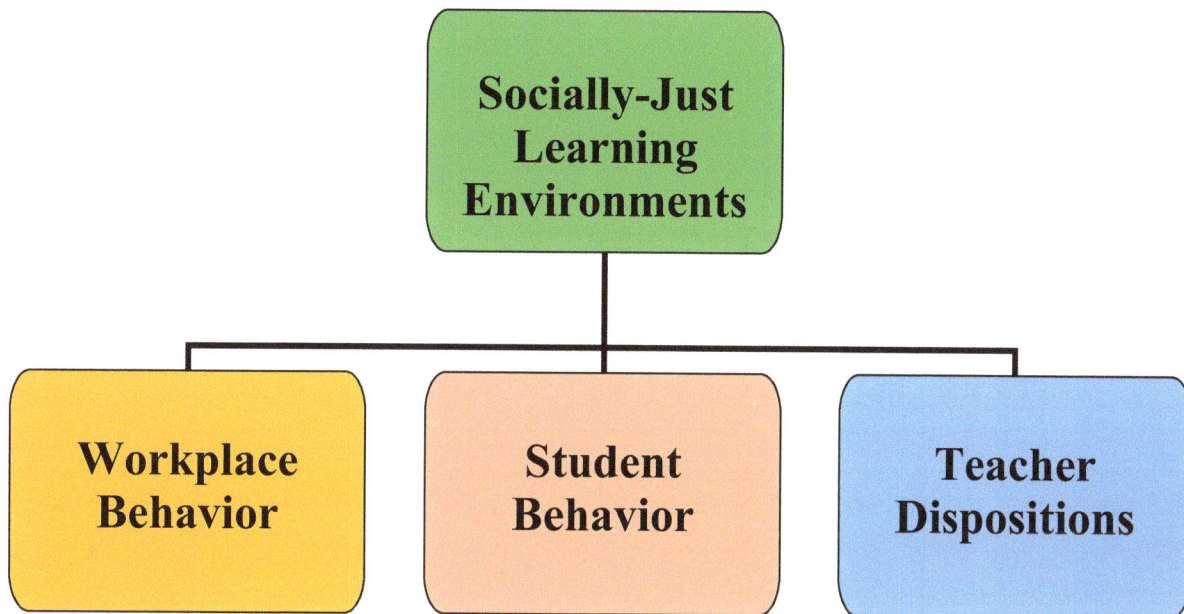

```
                  ┌───────────────────┐
                  │   Socially-Just   │
                  │     Learning      │
                  │   Environments    │
                  └───────────────────┘
        ┌──────────────────┼──────────────────┐
┌────────────────┐ ┌────────────────┐ ┌────────────────┐
│   Workplace    │ │    Student     │ │    Teacher     │
│    Behavior    │ │    Behavior    │ │  Dispositions  │
└────────────────┘ └────────────────┘ └────────────────┘
```

Teacher Dispositions: Focuses on targeting personal and professional worldviews and how implicit bias, sometimes, shapes teachers' dispositions, their personal views of students, and interactions with colleagues. These exercises heavily focus on self-reflection and self-evaluation.

Workplace behavior: Targets unethical behavior often displayed among colleagues while, also, pinpointing specific practices that can be used to build rapport between faculty and staff while remaining student-centered. These exercises address educator's decision-making skills.

Student Behavior: Works to explore students' dispositions and how their personal goals and needs largely impact their behavior in the classroom. Exercises highlight the evaluation and addressing of students' needs.

Socially-Just Learning Environments: Explores classroom practices used to build an equitable, enjoyable, and empowering school environment.

About the Creator

Jalesa D. Parks has been a strong advocate for social justice and education; therefore, she believes in providing safe spaces for those who are typically silenced such as minority people, students, and educators. Hence, she spends an immense amount of time exploring the lived experiences of underprivileged and underrepresented people. Her experience in the world of education is extensive, especially as it relates to innovative classroom practices, effective classroom management, and student advancement. Her career has expanded across secondary and post-secondary environments.

In the K-12 setting, Jalesa has taught 9th and 12th grade English. She has been recognized for her creative teaching practices and assignments, impeccable classroom management, and ability to connect with students from different backgrounds. As a result, she has been decorated with several awards and promotions, which included Professional Learning Community (PLC) leader, Advanced Placement coordinator and instructor, Dual Enrollment coordinator and instructor, and the Veteran of Foreign Wars (VFW) National Citizenship Education Teacher Award.

She has also taught at the collegiate level, with her social justice practices becoming a highlight among students and faculty. Therefore, she has been granted opportunities to facilitate several faculty seminars geared towards using technology in the classroom, implementing social justice to spark student engagement and activism, building an all-inclusive classroom and workplace environment, and promoting ethical behavior in the workplace. While teaching at a Historically Black College, she was the recipient of the 2019 Exemplary Teacher Award and the NAACP Angela Davis Humanitarian Award.

Furthermore, Jalesa has presented scholarly papers at several academic conferences such as the Association for Ethnic Studies (AES) 46th annual conference in Richmond, Virginia; International Conference on Urban Education (ICUE) in Nassau, Bahamas, and the American Association of Colleges for Teacher Education (AACTE) in Louisville, Kentucky. She, also, published *Tales of a First-Year Teacher*, which serves as a case study for new and veteran teachers looking to further build skills pertaining to workplace etiquette, classroom management, and teacher bias.

Jalesa holds a Master's degree in English and a Master's in Teaching, Secondary Education. In addition, she holds her doctorate in Educational Leadership and Policy Studies.

Personal Dimension

Contrary to popular belief, educators have personal lives outside of the school buildings in which they work. More often than not, their personal beliefs, values, and experiences shape their classroom behavior. These behaviors form what we call *Teacher Dispositions*, or your perceptions and attitudes that inform your interactions with students, colleagues, and the larger community.

Exercise 1: As you read Chapters 1-3 of *Tales of a First-Year Teacher*, pay close attention to the main character, Jada, and her actions. Using the lines below, make a list of observations you notice, as it relates to Jada's teacher dispositions and how they are impacted by her personal dimension.

Example: Jada relentlessly calls Caldwin High School to get a job. This shows her **strong-willed determination**, which she will likely bring into her classroom.

1. _____

_____

_____

2. _____

_____

_____

3. _____

_____

You might have noticed that Jada's personal dimension is impacted by both positive and negative attributes. Like Jada, all educators have beliefs, values, and behaviors that can positively and negatively impact the classroom. In order to be aware of these aspects, **self-reflection** is a vital component.

Exercise 2: Briefly reflect on your personal dimension. List positive and negative behaviors that may impact your teacher dispositions.

_____

_____

_____

_____

_____

_____

_____

_____

Before you Turn!

Use the numbers 1-4 to rank the puzzle pieces in order from least (4) to most (1) important in your life.

Friendliness

Organization

Passion

Loyalty

Exercise 3: Use the space below to reflect on one of the following components and what it means to you. (a) Friendliness (b) Passion (c) Organization (d) Loyalty.

LEADERSHIP

Theorist Warren G. Bennis (2009) argued that effective leaders are servants who coach, influence, and empower faculty and staff to participate in building positive and productive learning communities.

He, also, suggests that leaders use words and symbols to make ideas seem real and tangible to others.

Exercise 4: Read Chapter 4 of *Tales of a First-Year Teacher*. Then, answer the following questions:

Does Principal Jackson embody Bennis' leadership theory? Be sure to explain your answer.

_____

_____

_____

_____

_____

_____

_____

_____

_____

Would you want to work under Principal Jackson's leadership? Why or why not?

_____

_____

_____

_____

_____

_____

_____

_____

Does Ms. Calloway, the instructional facilitator, embody Bennis' leadership theory? Be sure to explain your answer.

_____

_____

_____

_____

_____

_____

_____

To Work or Not to Work... That is the Question.

Douglas McGregor (1966/1967) argues that in the workplace, two kinds of people exist. Those who enjoy working (Theory Y) and those who do not (Theory X).

Exercise 5: Proceed to Chapter 5 of *Tales of a First-Year Teacher*. Based on McGregor's theoretical lens, does Jada's actions align with Theory X or Theory Y? Be sure to explain your answer.

_____

_____

_____

_____

_____

_____

_____

_____

Exercise 6: Reflect on your own work ethic. Do you exhibit Theory X or Theory Y? Be sure to, also, include concrete examples of your work ethic.

_____

_____

_____

_____

_____

_____

_____

_____

The Four Temperaments

Oftentimes, the four temperaments are incorporated in education in order to understand individual's character. While these four temperaments should not be used to label people, they may provide further insight for people's behaviors and personal dispositions. A person may even go through each temperament in phases (Bobgan & Bobgan, 1992).

Exercise 7: Referring to Chapters 4 and 5, fill the blanks with the names of characters who exemplify each of the four temperaments. Reflect on your selections.

Choleric
- task-oriented, analytical, straightforward, unfriendly, loners, and small-talk avoiders

  - _____

  - _____

Sanguine
- optimistic, lively, adventurous, carefree, entertaining, and artsy

  - _____

  - _____

Melancholic
- traditional, thorough, family-oriented, deep thinkers, often feel misunderstood

  - _____

  - _____

Phlegmatic
- sociable, charitable, loyal, helpful, relationship-oriented, and ideal mediators

  - _____

  - _____

The Art of Storytelling

Humans tend to be complex. Therefore, we often look for a means by which to connect with people, their experiences, and the messages they intend to deliver. Storytelling has been used as both a social and cultural tool for relaying information and helping people fully interpret and digest messages. Researchers have found it to be extremely useful in the classroom.

Exercise 8: In Chapter 6, storytelling is used often. Identify two storytelling moments. Based on the identified moments, what are the benefits of storytelling? Write your response in the space below.

_____

_____

_____

_____

_____

_____

_____

_____

_____

_____

_____

_____

_____

_____

_____

_____

_____

_____

Assessing Students' Needs

Psychologist Abraham Maslow (1943) found that people have five distinct levels of needs. To reach the highest level of need, self-actualization, he argues that a person's most basic needs must be met.

Exercise 9: At this point in the novel, you have met Vanessa. In each of the spaces, assess Vanessa's needs. Has she reached each level of needs? If so, what information leads you to this assumption? If not, what steps can be taken to help her?

Physiological

- Basic needs such as food, shelter, and health

_____

_____

Safety

- The need for protection against dangers, attacks, and threats

_____

_____

Social

- The need for belonging and interpersonal relationships

_____

_____

Esteem

- Feeling valued, resilient, and self-sufficient

_____

_____

Self Actualization

- The desire to reach one's full potential

_____

_____

We began this workbook by discussing Teacher Dispositions, or perceptions, attitudes, and personal experiences that largely influence teacher's behaviors. The following exercises will further explore teacher's personal dimensions and the impact that their personal perceptions may or may not have on their behavior in the workplace.

Exercise 10: As you read Chapter 7, what does Jada's relationship with Caleb reveal about her?

_____

_____

_____

_____

_____

_____

_____

_____

_____

_____

_____

Exercise 11: Jada attends a dinner with her colleagues. Use the space below to assess the teacher and personal dispositions of the following characters.

Ms. Henson:_____

_____

_____

_____

_____

Ms. Calloway:_____

_____

_____

_____

Mr. Vincent:_____

_____

_____

_____

Jada Harris:_____

_____

_____

_____

Exercise 12: Read Chapter 8. In your opinion, is Mrs. Kimble's behavior ethical or unethical? Should Jada make Principal Jackson aware of Mrs. Kimble's actions? Be sure to explain your answers.

_____

_____

_____

_____

_____

_____

Exercise 13: Jada attends a parent-teacher conference. What was the primary purpose of the meeting? What does this meeting reveal about Jada?

_____

_____

_____

_____

_____

Exercise 14: Does Jada handle her encounter with Franklin correctly? If not, how could she have better handled the situation? Explain your answers.

_____

_____

_____

_____

_____

_____

Interactive Classroom Practices

Researchers suggest that teachers implement practices that appeal to the "whole child," ensuring that students are (a) engaged (b) secured (c) challenged (d) fully supported (Darling-Hammond & Cook-Harvey, 2018).

Exercise 15: Does Jada's classroom activity in Chapter 9 align with researchers' concept of the *whole child*? Would you incorporate a similar activity? Be sure to explain your answers.

_____

_____

_____

_____

_____

_____

_____

_____

_____

_____

_____

_____

_____

_____

_____

_____

_____

_____

_____

Public Appearances vs. Private Realities

Psychologist Mark Snyder (1987) argued that people possess a public appearance, or a particular persona that they display to the outside world, while, also, maintaining a private reality, or who they are in actuality.

Exercise 16: Continue reading Chapters 9 and 10. Write about one character's public and private selves in the space provided below.

Character:_____

Public Appearances	Private Realities

VS

Reflect on your own public appearances and private realities. What attributes do you display in public? What do you keep private? Should you consider rearranging these characteristics, making some private and others more public?

Leadership Styles

Robert House and Terence Mitchell (1974) defined four types of leader behavior.

Supportive Leadership	**Directive Leadership**
<ul><li>Approachable</li><li>Builds a pleasant work environment</li><li>Takes others into consideration</li><li>Shows genuine concern for others' needs</li></ul>	<ul><li>Makes expectations clear</li><li>Sets goals/standards</li><li>Informs faculty of tasks</li><li>Offers specific directions</li></ul>
Participative Leadership	**Achievement-Oriented Leadership**
<ul><li>Follows up with faculty and staff on job-related matters</li><li>Promotes shared decision-making</li></ul>	<ul><li>Places stellar performance at the forefront</li><li>Sets challenging goals</li><li>Shows confidence in faculty and staff abilities</li></ul>

Exercise 17: Which of the four types of leader behavior does Principal Jackson display in Chapters 11 and 12? Which kind of leader do you find suitable for your teaching needs? Be sure to support your answers with concrete examples from the text.

_____

_____

_____

_____

_____

_____

_____

Oh, How Our Worlds Turn...

Exercise 18: Read Chapter 13. Reflect on Jada's journey up until this point. Has she evolved as a person and teacher? Explain your answer.

_____

_____

_____

_____

_____

_____

_____

_____

Exercise 19: After reading Chapter 14, list 5 standards that should govern the behavior of all school leaders and educators. These should be standards that you deem necessary for the characters in *Tales of a First-Year Teacher* as well.

1._____

_____

2._____

_____

3._____

_____

4._____

_____

5._____

_____

Exercise 20: Read Chapter 15. Is Jada's reaction justified? Are Ashton's parents justified? Does Coach Lewis make the best decision? Explain your answers below.

_____

_____

_____

_____

_____

_____

_____

_____

_____

> Teacher bias refers to the stereotypical beliefs that educators develop about their students. They are typically reflections of one's upbringing or personal beliefs and values. While they may lay dormant for a while, it is only a matter of time before they come to the surface, negatively impacting students.

Exercise 21: Read Chapter 16. What biases, if any, are evident in Mrs. Barnes' actions?

_____

_____

_____

_____

_____

_____

SPOILER AHEAD!!

STOP

READ CHAPTERS 17 AND 18, THEN COMPLETE THE FOLLOWING EXERCISES!!!

Exercise 22: Researchers Hummer, Crosland, and Dollard (2009) found four steps that can be used to address trauma. They are as follows:

- **To Connect** by highlighting relationships
- **To Offer Protection** by creating an atmosphere of safety and honesty
- **To Promote Respect** by collaborating and engaging in choice rather than obligation
- **To Redirect** through skill-building

In Chapter 17, does Ms. Henson and the school faculty properly address the traumatic aftermath experienced by the students? Be sure to explain your answer.

_____

_____

_____

_____

_____

_____

_____

Exercise 23: Is there anyone to blame for this traumatic experience? Explain.

_____

_____

_____

_____

_____

_____

Signing the Dotted Line...

Exercise 24: Reflect on the feelings/emotions you experienced while reading *Tales of a First-Year Teacher*. Make a list of questions or specific and/or general statements that you have now that you have completed the book.

_____

_____

_____

_____

_____

_____

_____

Exercise 25: Based on the reading, your reflections, and your responses to each question, develop an official mantra that you intend to abide by as an educator.

_____

_____

_____

_____

_____

_____

_____

_____

Bibliography

Bennis, W. (2009). *On becoming a leader*. New York: Basic Books.

Bobgan, D. and Bobgan, M. (1992). *Christians and the four temperaments theory*. Santa
  Barbara, California: EastGate Publishers.

Darling-Hammond, L., & Cook-Harvey, C.M. (2018). *Educating the whole child: Improving
  school climate to support student success*. Palo Alto, CA: Learning Policy Institute.
  https://learningpolicyinstitute.org/product/educating-whole-child-report

House, R.J., & Mitchell, T.R. (1974). Path-goal theory of leadership. *Journal of Contemporary
  Business, 3*: 1-97.

Hummer, V.L., Crosland, K., & Dollard, N. (2009). Applied behavioral analysis within a trauma-
  informed framework. Presented at the Florida Center for Inclusive Communities
  'Lunch 'n Learn' Series. Tampa, FL.

Maslow, A.H. (1943). A theory of human motivation. *Psychological Review, 50*(4), 370-96.

McGregor, D.M. (1967). *The professional manager*. Eds. W.G. Bennis and C. McGregor.
  New York, NY: McGraw-Hill.

———1966. *Leadership and motivation*. Cambridge, MA: MIT Press.

———1960/1985. *The human side of enterprise*. New York, NY: McGraw-Hill.

Snyder, M. (1987). *A series of books in psychology. Public appearances, private realities: The
  psychology of self-monitoring*. New York, NY: W.H. Freeman/Times Books/Henry Holt
  & Co.

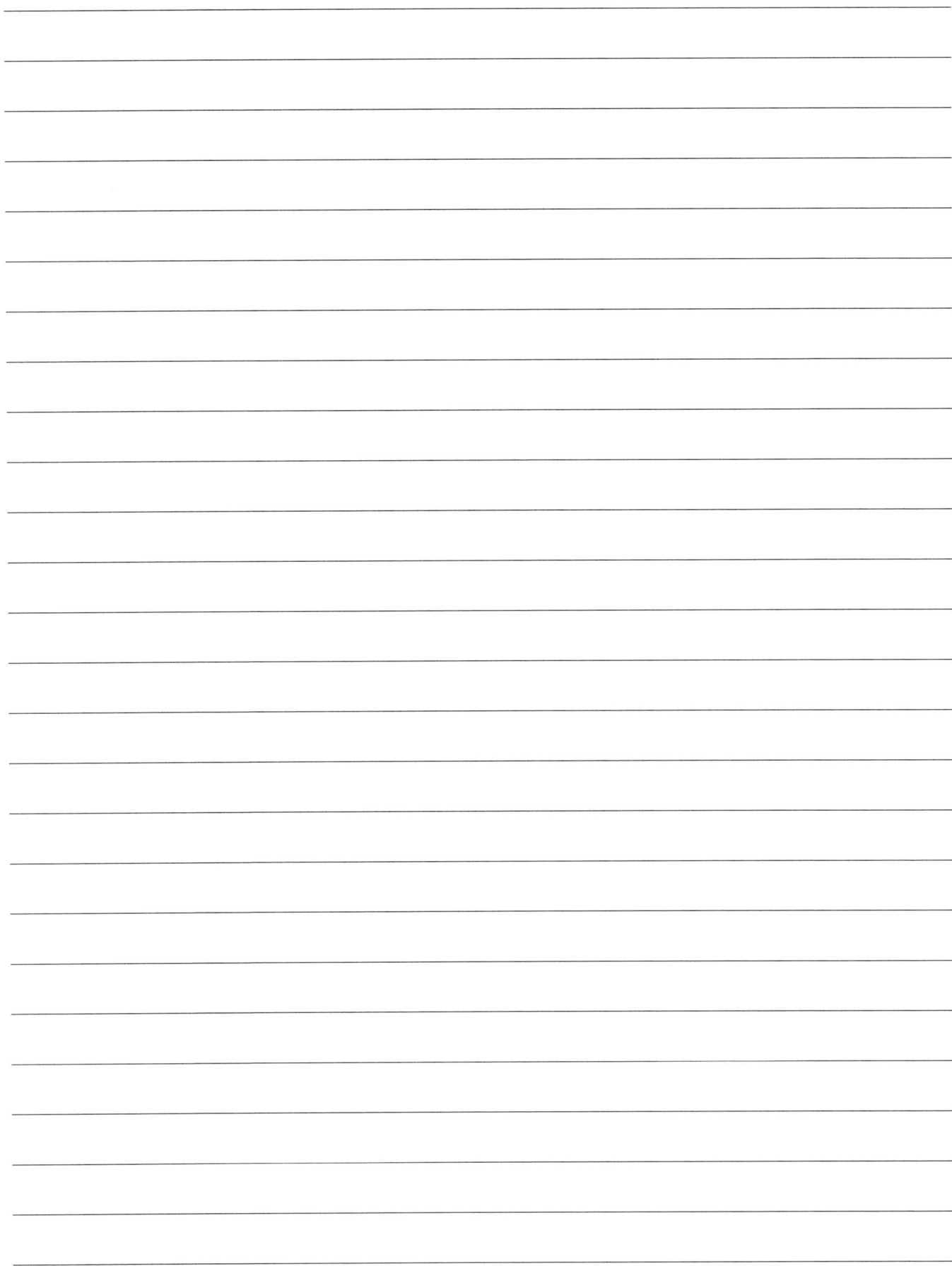

www.ingramcontent.com/pod-product-compliance
Lightning Source LLC
Chambersburg PA
CBHW040019050426
42452CB00002B/47